Drinking
Games

DOG 'n' BONE

Drinking Games

One book, 25 games, just add booze

Dominic Bliss

DOG 'n' BONE

Published in 2012 by Dog 'n' Bone Books
An imprint of Ryland Peters & Small Ltd.
20–21 Jockey's Fields   519 Broadway, 5th Floor
London WC1R 4BW   New York, NY 10012

www.dogandbonebooks.com

10 9 8 7 6 5 4 3 2 1

Text © Dominic Bliss 2012
Design and photography © Dog 'n' Bone Books 2012

A CIP catalog record for this book is available from the
Library of Congress and the British Library.

ISBN: 978 0 957140 94 3

Printed in China

Editor: Pete Jorgensen
Designer: Ashley Western
Illustration: Kuo Kang Chen except for pages 8 (bottom left), 11, and 15
by Stephen Dew

For digital editions, visit www.cicobooks.com/apps.php

Contents

Introduction

Drinking games have been around as long as there's been drinking. In fact, it's highly likely Neanderthals used to sit around their caves on winter evenings and pass the time by goading each other into munching on tons of fermented fruit.

Fortunately, nowadays, we don't have to rely on half-rotten apples to get our kicks. And after eons of ritual drinking, we've developed some classic games to ease the passage of booze down our throats. This book brings together the best of those classic games, plus many rather unusual ones.

Forfeits

Most drinking games require players to complete a task. Failure in that task results in a drinking forfeit. The strength of this forfeit should depend on the constitution of the players. There's no point making each forfeit three shots of vodka, unless you want the evening to end especially quickly.

Easy forfeits might be a finger of beer (i.e. a slug of beer equivalent to the thickness of your finger against the side of the glass). Dangerous forfeits might be large shots of liquor or whole glasses of beer. Drinking games normally work best if they feature lots of little drinks over a long evening.

Tough luck if you happen to have very fat fingers.

The Games

Beer Hunter

Players: two to six

Equipment: a six-pack of beer

Hangover potential: two

Skill: zero

Remember that scary scene in the 1970s Vietnam War film, *The Deer Hunter*, when Robert De Niro and Christopher Walken are forced to play Russian roulette in a Viet Cong prison camp? Well, this is almost as extreme, except you replace guns with cans of beer, and enemy soldiers with your drinking comrades. Oh, and play it outside if you don't want to ruin the carpet.

Place a six-pack of beer on the table. Shake up one of the cans extra vigorously and shuffle it up among the other cans so that no player knows which has been shaken. Each player then chooses a can, holds it right up close to his or her face, and pulls the tab. One player ends up being doused with beer, while the other five emerge unscathed.

As additional punishment, the player fresh from the beer shower has to down an extra can of beer.

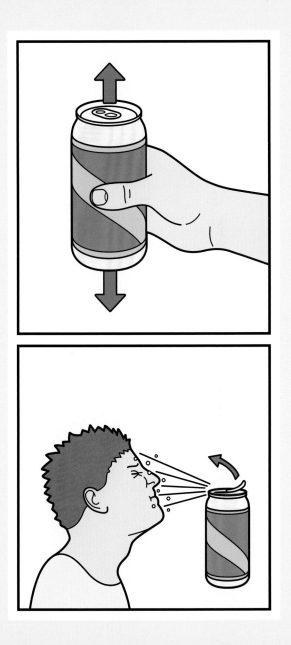

Blind Barman

Players: three or more

Equipment: a pack of cards and a well-stocked bar

Hangover potential: four

Skill: one

Ever struggle to create the perfect cocktail? With this game you can throw caution to the wind since you'll end up mixing some of the most revolting concoctions known to man.

Line up as many liquors and mixers on the table as you can possibly find. Next, lay a pack of cards face down on the table. Each player takes turns picking up a card. The first one to pick up a king gets to choose the liquor. The second king chooses the mixer. Then—yes, you guessed it—the third king gets to down the impromptu cocktail. Just like it's been mixed by a blind barman.

Whisky and tomato juice, anyone? How about a delicious mix of crème de menthe and pineapple? To really spice things up, include the two jokers in the pack. Pick those up and you have to drink a double dose.

Last Card

👫 **Players:** two or more

🍺 **Equipment:** a pack or cards and a bottle of wine

➕ **Hangover potential:** three

🏃 **Skill:** four

This game tests both your drinking prowess and your coordination.

Place a full pack of cards on top of a wine bottle. Players then take turns in putting their mouth up close to the pack of cards and trying to blow just a few of the cards off the top of the pack. Whoever ends up blowing the final card off the bottle has to down a glass of wine.

Of course, it's all about finding a happy middle ground. Blow too softly and it could take 52 blows before the drinker is finally allocated. Blow too hard and you'll tumble the entire pack straight away. Of course, the fun part is that the more you drink, the harder it is to blow with any degree of accuracy.

Liquid Legends

Booze and firearms never mix. Unless you're in the British army, that is. Apparently, a favorite drinking game involves two officers, a bike, a shotgun, some light shot, and a bottle of port. The two protagonists start off by flipping a coin. The loser immediately jumps on the bike and pedals off as fast as possible, while the winner necks the port, loads the gun, and tries to shoot his opponent in the back.

Liquid Legends

One of the biggest boozing celebrities of all time was actor Oliver Reed. He once claimed to have drunk over 100 pints of beer in two days before marrying his second wife Josephine. Reed died in 1999 after a night of hard drinking and arm wrestling.

Ozzy Osbourne

Players: three or more

Equipment: a good knowledge of famous people

Hangover potential: three

Skill: four

Like all the best games, this one is deceptively easy to start off with, but rapidly becomes very tricky. Sit in a circle and allocate a player to start. All he or she has to do is state the name of someone famous. Any celebrity will do, real or fictitious, from pop star to politician, actor to astronaut, just as long as other players have heard of them.

The next player has just five seconds to name another famous person whose first name begins with first letter of the last name of the previous celebrity. So, James Bond might beget Britney Spears. Britney Spears might beget Saddam Hussein—now there's a scary thought! The game carries on in a clockwise direction unless someone says a name that's alliterative—such as Ozzy Osbourne or Tina Turner—in which case you switch directions and the player who went previously has to go again.

Fail to say a name within five seconds, and you drink. Fabricate a name or get it wrong (other players can challenge you), and you drink. Repeat a name that's already been said, and—yes—it's time to drink. It's surprising how quickly you run out of memorable celebrities to use.

Flip, Sip, or Strip

Players: three or more

Equipment: a coin and a full set of clothes

Hangover potential: three

Skill: one

This is the ultimate ice-breaker since it involves both drinking and stripping.

Sit in a circle. Each player takes turn flipping a coin. Guess heads or tails correctly and you pass the coin clockwise for someone else to flip. Guess wrong, however, and you have two options: either drink or remove an item of clothing.

Most players spend the first half of the game going for the drinking option. Then, as inebriation sets in, they spend the second half on the stripping option. Much like an average evening in a bar, then.

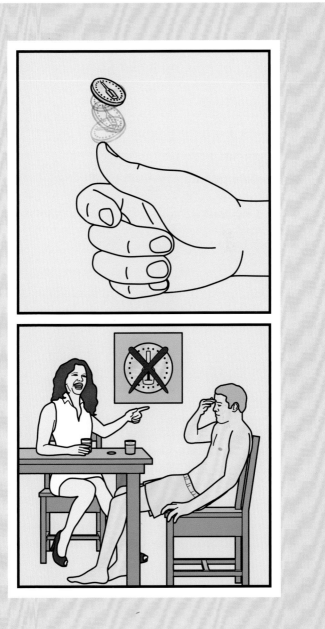

This side you drink

5 4 3 2 1

This side they drink

Ice-cube Tray

👫 **Players:** two or more

🍺 **Equipment:** an ice-cube tray and a coin

➕ **Hangover potential:** three

🏃 **Skill:** four

There comes a time in every evening when all the ice runs out. It's no good sitting there, staring at the refrigerator, willing it to freeze more ice cubes. You can put that ice-cube tray to much better use by playing this drinking game.

Place the tray (one with between 10 and 14 cubes works well) in front of you on the table. You now have to bounce a coin off the table and into the tray. Keep bouncing until you successfully land the coin inside one of the sections. If it lands on the left-hand column of the tray, you can nominate someone else to drink. Land one in the right-hand column and you must drink yourself. The number of finger measures to be drunk are determined by how far into the tray the coin lands: the cube nearest to you means one finger measure; the second cube means two finger measures; and so on, right up to a maximum of seven.

Buzz Fizz

Players: three or more

Equipment: a mathematics degree

Hangover potential: three

Skill: five

If mathematics is your weak subject, avoid this game like the plague. Poor mathematicians are even poorer when there's booze on board.

Sit in a circle and take turns counting upwards from one. (So far, even a math reject can handle it.) Things start to get tricky when you reach five, however. The rule is that any number divisible by five, or that contains a five, must be replaced by the word "buzz." Likewise, any number divisible by seven, or that contains a seven, is replaced by the word "fizz." Miss a buzz or a fizz and you have to drink. (And watch out for numbers that are divisible by both five and seven, or which contain both a five and a seven. They must be called out as "buzz fizz" or "fizz buzz.")

Apparently this game is very popular with university mathematics students. There's an urban legend that a bunch of geeks once reached well over 1,000 before someone made a mistake. Mere mortals will do well to get past 100.

Liquid Legends

Ancient Greeks used to play a drinking game called kottabus. Players would yell out the name of the woman they loved while throwing the last remaining drops of wine from their cup into a metal bowl in the middle of the floor. If the drops landed right in the bowl, then a promising love affair was on the cards. If they missed, then it meant the goddess of love had rejected them.

Liquid Legends

Ancient Viking King Håkon took his country's Christmas celebrations very seriously. All his subjects were forced to drink ale throughout the entire holiday. Those who refused were fined.

Marlboro Man

👥 **Players:** three or more

🍺 **Equipment:** a pack of smokes

➕ **Hangover potential:** three

🏃 **Skill:** four

Smokers are so anti-social, what with nipping outside every 10 minutes for a crafty smoke. This game will ensure they remain in the thick of the action.

The idea is to take turns throwing a packet of cigarettes over your beer glass and onto the table. Land the packet on its largest surface and you immediately drink. But land it on its side, or its end, and the person next to you must drink one or three finger measures respectively. The only way he or she can avoid this is by again throwing the packet onto its side or end, in which case the forfeit increases incrementally and is passed onto the third player. Should the packet land flat at any time, then that player has to drink the accumulated forfeit.

Skilled cigarette-packet throwers can very quickly accumulate a massive forfeit for their opponents.

Edward Ciderhands

Players: two or more

Equipment: bottles of cider and duct tape

Hangover potential: four

Skill: one

There's no bailing out of this game halfway through. You're fully committed until every last drop of liquid has been drunk.

Everyone needs two large-ish bottles of cider (you could also use beer bottles, or even wine bottles for a game of Amy Winehands) and an enormous roll of duct tape. Get someone to strap an open bottle of cider to each of your hands using the tape. (It's about now that you suddenly realize why the game's called Edward Ciderhands.) Once everyone's fully taped up, you then embark on a drinking game. Pretty much any game will do, as long as it doesn't require hands—Buzz Fizz (page 22), Ozzy Osbourne (page 17), or perhaps Roxanne (page 33) would all work well. The only extra rule is that you can't remove the taped bottles until they're both empty. Not even to go to the bathroom.

Rumor has it Johnny Depp loves this game. Plays it with his buddies every week.

Battleships

Players: two or more

Equipment: beers, a tumbler, and a beer pitcher

Hangover potential: four

Skill: three

A favorite of frat parties, this one. And a great way to get soaked in beer if you pour too fast.

Fill a pitcher halfway up with beer. Then place a small tumbler glass inside it so that it floats upright. (You may have to pour a little beer inside the tumbler to stop it capsizing straight away.) Now players take turns pouring beer from their own glasses into the tumbler. Whoever sinks the glass has to drink the entire contents of the pitcher. While you have to be wary not to fill the glass up too much when it comes to your turn, at the same time you need to fill it up just enough so that you don't end up running the gauntlet a second time.

James Bond

Players: two or more

Equipment: a DVD/Blu-ray player and a Bond movie

Hangover potential: four

Skill: two

The perfect drinking game for couch potatoes. Simply mix up a huge round of vodka martinis, pop a Bond movie into the DVD player (any one will do), and sit back and wait for the fun to begin.

The rules are fairly simple, and you can adapt them according to everyone's ability to hold their liquor. Every time someone dies, you all take a sip; easy if you're watching the rather sedate *Dr. No*, but rather tricky if you have a high-body-count movie such as *You Only Live Twice*—91 deaths, last time we checked. The same goes for vehicle explosions and any time 007 is mentioned.

It's up to you and your friends to decide on other forfeits. You might suggest compulsory drinking every time Bond flirts with Miss Moneypenny, for example; or every time he delivers a punch; or when he appears in a tuxedo. The options are endless.

There are two scenarios, however, when your martini must be drained right to the bottom of the glass. That's whenever the immortal line: "The name's Bond… James Bond" is uttered. Or whenever Bond orders a vodka martini "shaken, not stirred."

The genius of this game is that you can adapt it to any movie franchise you like—*Star Wars*, *Harry Potter*, *Batman*, *Rocky*, *Toy Story*. Just change the forfeits to suit. Be warned, the body count in *Toy Story* is disappointingly low.

Liquid Legends

Alexander the Great was one of history's most prodigious
drinkers. He once organized an Olympic Games to honor
a dead Indian religious leader. However, since the Indians
weren't familiar with Greek sport, he opted for a wine-
drinking contest instead. 41 contestants died during the
Games, and the winner lived just four days after his victory.

Roxanne

Players: two or more

Equipment: a compilation album of The Police and a music player

Hangover potential: three

Skill: one

Singing and drinking have always gone hand in hand, but this 1978 song by The Police involves more drinking than you quite bargain for. To play, just stick The Police's *Greatest Hits* on the stereo, and key up "Roxanne."

There's one rule: every time the band sings "Roxanne," you have to take a big sip. Of course, it all starts out rather easy, as the famous lady of the night's name comes up just once every three lines. But, like all the best drinking games, the pressure builds up exponentially. First, the chorus kicks in, then after a short reprise for the second verse, you have the final coda, during which Roxanne's name is repeated ad infinitum.

Be warned. In all, there are well over 25 Roxannes to contend with in just over three minutes. So, it might be best to put the vodka bottle down and stick to beer or wine.

Sports Bar

Players: four or more

Equipment: a TV

Hangover potential: four

Skill: one

The trouble with watching sports on TV is that it gets in the way of good drinking time. The answer, of course, is to combine the two. And the best thing is that you can play this game with any sport, from baseball or football to tennis or tiddlywinks. Just make sure you agree the rules before you start.

Split the group into two teams, and allocate a sports team to each drinking team. Now decide on the forfeits. For example, if you're watching soccer on TV, you may have to down a shot every time there's a corner kick or a throw-in. Triple measures every time your team scores a goal. With baseball it might be a shot for every strikeout, and a triple shot for catches and home runs.

Trust me, this will liven up even the most boring sports. Just don't choose test cricket. The drinking game ends only when the sports game is over. With cricket you could be playing for days, and even after all that the final result might be a draw.

Liquid Legends

Impress your friends. Learn how to say "Cheers" in unusual languages: Kippis (Finland); Sláinte (Irish Gaelic); Kanpai (Japanese); Serefe (Turkish); Budmo (Ukrainian); Prieka (Latvian); Prost (German).

Boat Race

Players: multiples of two

Equipment: pint glasses

Hangover potential: three

Skill: three

Ivy Leaguers and Oxford and Cambridge University students particularly love this game. Split everyone into two equal teams. Ideally, if you want to remain true to the sport, there should be four or eight on each team. Now each team sits down on the floor, in a line, as if they're all rowers in two boats. Everyone has a full pint of beer in their hand. To spice things up, place yourselves boy-girl-boy-girl with your legs around the person in front of you.

On the word "Go," the bowman, at the front of the boat, starts to neck his beer. As soon as he's downed it all, he places the empty glass on top of his head, at which point the rower behind him embarks on her pint. The game continues in the same shipshape fashion until both strokes, at the back of each boat, have downed their pints. Each member of the losing team has to down an extra pint as a forfeit.

Chicken Feed

Players: multiples of two plus one umpire

Equipment: a long table and two packs of cards

Hangover potential: three

Skill: two

This has to be the most chaotic drinking game there is. It's certainly not for the faint-hearted. You might even call it a blood sport!

Split up into two teams, with each team on the opposite side of a long table. One person—the one who is least fond of contact sports is a good choice—volunteers to be umpire.

Now scatter one pack of cards, all face up, randomly across the table. The other pack goes to the umpire who proceeds to read out, one by one, each card in his or her pack. Every time the umpire names a card, all the players quickly scan the table to locate the same card in their own pack. Then, using just one finger on one hand, they attempt to drag that particular card off their side of the table while opposing players try to do the very same thing. If they succeed, everyone on the opposing team has to drink. With 52 cards to get through, the game gets rather feisty toward the latter stages.

It's not difficult to imagine the carnage that ensues, which is why the umpire must insist on some strict rules. To win the card, the team must drag only the correct card off the table each time—more than one card and it's declared null. Only one finger on one hand can be used. Players are allowed to use their finger to hook an opposing player's finger off the card.

Watch out for players with sharp fingernails!

Bar Golf

Players: four or more

Equipment: lots of bars in close proximity

Hangover potential: five

Skill: one

This classic bar-crawl game involves either a nine-hole or 18-hole course, depending on your group's capacity and stamina. Nine holes, of course, means nine different bars have to be visited. 18 holes means 18 different bars.

Assign a team captain before you start. It's his or her job to choose the type of drink for each bar. A friendly word of warning: if you're gunning for 18 holes, you may want to stick to beer! In each bar (or hole), all players must attempt to down their drinks in as few gulps as possible. Scoring is the same as in real golf: fewer gulps mean a higher score. The winner is the player with the least number of swigs by the end of the round.

To make the game more realistic, insist that everyone dresses in extra-loud golfing attire: plus fours, Argyll sweaters, caps, gloves—the whole nine yards.

Beer Pong with paddles

👥 **Players:** multiples of two
🍺 **Equipment:** glasses, two paddles, and ping pong balls
➕ **Hangover potential:** two
🏃 **Skill:** four

This could be an Olympic sport one day. Well, if synchronized swimming qualifies, why not this game?

If playing with two players, take your positions at either end of a table tennis table. Place three half-full, but large, glasses of beer on your side of the table. Put them anywhere you like, but not next to the net. Now start playing table tennis, but, instead of winning points, you attempt to hit the ping pong ball into your opponent's glasses. Clip one of the glasses with the ball and he or she has to down a finger measure. Land the ball right in the glass and the glass has to be drained. Whichever player ends up with three empty glasses first has to drain all the remaining beer on the table. And don't worry if you don't have a table tennis table. Any large rectangular table will work; just fashion a makeshift net out of something—hockey sticks and broom handles will usually do the trick.

This game works as singles, doubles, triples... anything that's a multiple of two. For larger games the same rules apply, the only difference being that once the first team member has played a shot the rest of the teammates follow until a glass is hit. If you want to make the game more interesting, add a few more glasses to the table.

Beer Pong
the hands-only version

Players: multiples of two
Equipment: at least 12 plastic cups, ping pong balls, and a large table
Hangover potential: four
Skill: five

Even if you don't have a table tennis table, you can play this game on any large table.

Start by positioning three cups at each end of the table. In front of these place another two, then one more to make a triangle shape. Fill each of the cups on your side with beer apart from one; save this for a delectable concoction of your choice… Baileys and lime juice perhaps? Repeat on the other side.

Now divide your friends into two sides and gather each team at opposite ends of the table. A member of the first team starts the game by attempting to throw a ball into one of the cups at the opposite end of the table. This can be done in two ways: either by bouncing the ball onto the table and into a cup or by throwing it in an arc. When the ball lands in the cup, a player on the opposing team must down the contents and remove it from the table. The second team now has the chance to return the favor and the game carries on until one side has hit the target on all eight cups. The losing team has to down all the cups left on the winners' side, plus an extra drink of the victors' choice.

There are a lot of local variations of this game—for example, some players add an extra row or two of cups, whilst others allow you to swat the ball away if it bounces on their side of the table. Try experimenting with your own rules and forfeits.

Coin Football

Players: two

Equipment: a square or rectangular table and a coin

Hangover potential: four

Skill: four

Stand at either end of the table. Place the coin so it overlaps the edge of your end of the table. Then, using your finger to flick, move the coin across the table toward your opponent's edge. You have three flicks or fewer to get the coin to overlap his end of the table. Touchdown! Fail, and you drink. Succeed, and you must walk round to your competitor's side of the table, flick the coin from its overlapping position up into the air, and catch it. Again, drink if you fail; proceed if you succeed.

Let's presume you succeed. Now return to your side of the table and, using two fingers, spin the coin hard on the table surface. Before it stops spinning, attempt to trap it between your two thumbs. Once again, drink if you fail; proceed if you succeed.

The final section of the game is the field goal. Your opponent makes the shape of goalposts with his hands on his side of the table. You, meanwhile, use the thumbs you've just trapped the coin with to flick the coin over the posts. Fail and you drink again. Succeed and your opponent has to down his entire drink.

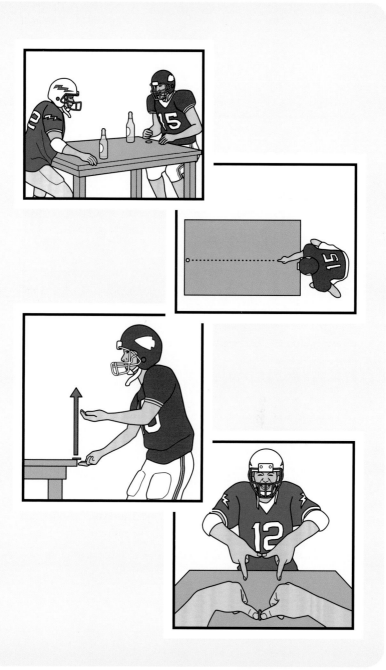

Liquid Legends
Early Anglo-Saxons often used to drink out of vessels made of cattle horns. The idea was that they couldn't be put down until they were completely empty.

Monkeys

Players: as many as possible

Equipment: lots of furniture

Hangover potential: three

Skill: one

You know those cold, winter evenings when everyone settles down for a nice, quiet drink in front of the fire? Well, this game is definitely not for fans of those kind of nights.

It's best played in a large group, while drinking at a busy bar. Without warning, one of the group will yell out "Monkeys!" at the top of his or her voice, at which point everyone must immediately avoid touching the ground. They can jump up on the bar, kneel on a chair, or leap onto a table—anywhere, in fact, as long as no part of their body is touching the ground. The last person to achieve the monkey position has to drain a drink. This player then has the privilege of being the next person to shout out "Monkeys!"

The game's even better played outdoors at barbecues.

Ring of Fire

Players: four or more

Equipment: a pack of cards

Hangover potential: five

Skill: one

Randomly scatter a pack of cards face down on the table. Players now take turns to pick up a card with the following consequences:

2, 3, or 4: The player downs the appropriate finger measures of booze.

5: Last player to raise a hand for a high five has to drink.

6: Last player to place a thumb on the table has to drink.

7: The player to the left has to drink.

8: The player to the right has to drink.

9: The player opposite you has to drink.

10: The player nominates a victim to drink.

Jack: All the boys have to drink.

Queen: All the girls have to drink.

King: The player has to drain his or her drink.

Ace: Everyone has to drain their drinks.

Feel free to modify the rules, or up the ante, as you see fit.

Liquid Legends

Humans have been making alcoholic drinks for at least the last 9,000 years. In northern China, archaeologists have found pottery jars containing the remnants of fermented rice, honey, grapes, and hawthorn berries.

Nut Race

Players: two or more

Equipment: beer glasses and a bag of nuts

Hangover potential: three

Skill: one

Didn't your mother always warn you not to drink on an empty stomach? While this drinking game hardly fills you up, it does actually involve solids as well as liquids.

Each player holds a peanut eight inches above his or her full glass of beer and drops it in at exactly the same time. At first the peanut sinks to the bottom of the glass, as you'd expect. But within a few seconds—hey presto!—it starts to rise. The player whose peanut resurfaces last has to down a glass of beer and munch the peanut.

Make sure you use a whole peanut. Half peanuts will sink without trace.

Arrows of Death

👥 **Players:** three or more

🍺 **Equipment:** darts and a dart board, plus shot glasses

➕ **Hangover potential:** four

🏃 **Skill:** five

A dart board throws up all sorts of possibilities when it comes to drinking games, but the best ones tend to be the simplest.

For Arrows of Death, each player is allocated a number on the dart board and a shot glass. Taking turns, the players then attempt to throw a dart into their number section, downing a shot each time they are successful. If they hit the double ring, they down two shots; the treble ring, and it's three shots. Play continues until all the players have downed 10 shots.

But hold on. As ever, there are a few cheeky little rules which might bring out a player's vindictive streak. If you hit someone else's number, he or she has to down an extra shot as a forfeit. Doubles and trebles increase this forfeit. Should you miss the board altogether, your forfeit is to down an extra shot. Hit the outer bull and you can nominate someone to drink an extra shot. Hit the bull's eye and everyone has to down an extra shot.

Ever wondered why professional darts players are so fat? Here's your answer: copious amounts of booze.

Liquid Legends

Lots of beer can kill you, whether you actually drink it or not, as this cautionary tale reveals. In 1814, at the Meux & Company Brewery, in London, a huge vat of beer split open, causing a domino effect which ruptured all the other vats alongside it. In the resulting flood, 323,000 gallons of beer gushed onto the London streets, killing eight people in nearby basement homes.

Liquid Legends

The Scots have always had a reputation for being big drinkers. Little surprise then that, on remote Scottish islands, archaeologists have found Neolithic 30-gallon jars containing fermented barley and oats, but with a few extra hallucinogenic treatss thrown in, such as deadly nightshade and hemlock.

Who Am I?

Players: three or more
Equipment: pens and Post-it notes
or cigarette rolling papers
Hangover potential: four
Skill: four

Everyone writes the name of a celebrity, either real or a fictitious character, on a Post-it note or a cigarette rolling paper. They then stick the paper onto the forehead of the player to their left so that everyone can see the name except for the person wearing it.

Each player now tries to discover the identity of his or her celebrity by asking the other players questions—for example, "Am I a man? Am I an actor?" etc. However, answers are restricted to "yes" or "no." Every time there's a "no" answer, the questioner has to drink a finger measure. As soon as they guess their celebrity correctly, everyone else has to down their drinks.

Wine Checkers

Players: two

Equipment: 24 shot glasses and a checkers board

Hangover potential: four

Skill: three

There's an old adage among drinkers: stick to the same color wine and you'll avoid a hangover. Of course, that rule stops applying once you start consuming bacchanalian quantities of wine, but it's a good adage all the same.

For this game of two players, you need to choose whether red or white wine is your tipple. Fill up 12 shot glasses with white wine and 12 with red. Now use the checkers board for a regular game of checkers with just two slight rule changes: substitute the checkers for the shot glasses and every time you jump a shot glass, your opponent has to drink it.

Should you manage to crown one of your shot glasses king, swap it for a larger glass and fill it up with extra wine.

Be prepared for a very sticky checkers board, and a very messy game of checkers.

Cereal Killer

Players: four or more
Equipment: an empty cereal packet and a pair of scissors
Hangover potential: three
Skill: two

You know that Caribbean favorite, limbo dancing? This is the drinking-game equivalent. Crank up the music, stretch your limbs, and get ready to party.

Start off by placing a large, empty cereal box on the floor. Players now take it in turns to pick up the box with just their mouth. The problem is they're not allowed to touch the floor with any part of their body except their feet. (Usual drink forfeits apply, see page 7.) The other problem is that after each successful oral pick-up, a section must be sliced off the top of the cereal box, so it gradually gets shorter and shorter after each turn. Carry on playing until all you're left with is a shallow box just a couple of inches off the floor.

It won't be long before the drinking forfeits are coming thick and fast.

Blind Relay

Players: multiples of two

Equipment: beer bottles, a large table, and two blindfolds

Hangover potential: three

Skill: two

This is just like the 4x100 meter relay race, except you're all blind, and, if you play it long enough, blind drunk.

Split into two teams. Place several opened bottles of beer on a table at the far end of the room. Players now take turns negotiating their leg of the relay. This involves wearing a blindfold and being spun around 10 times before running across the room. When they reach the table they must grab a bottle of beer and down it as quickly as possible before running back to their team. The relay continues until all players have downed a beer and successfully navigated their way back to the start.

The losing team has to drink any remaining beers.

Acknowledgments

Thanks to all my fellow drinkers who, over the years, have (perhaps too) thoroughly tested many of these games with me. Especially Sally, Jez, Naytin, Lucy, Oli, Weeve, Dave, Muzzer, Adam, Dom, Tash, Chaz, and Caz.